·29·
MISSING

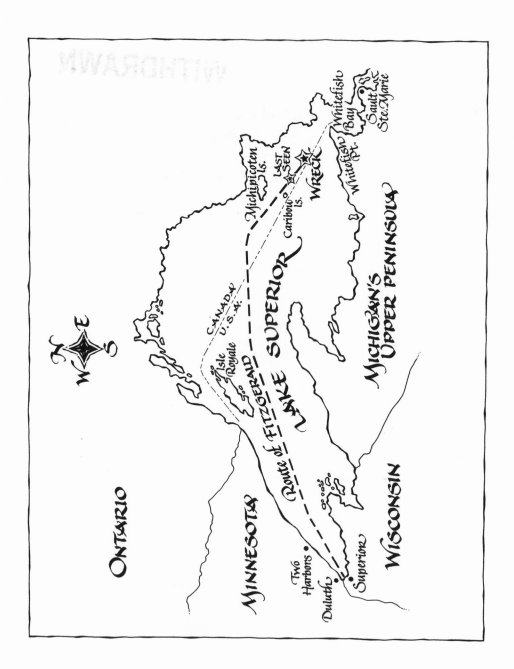

ONTARIO

MINNESOTA

Two
Harbors •

Duluth •

• Superior

WISCONSIN

Route of Fitzgerald

LAKE SUPERIOR

Isle
Royale

CANADA
U.S.A.

Michipicoten
Is.

Caribou
Is.

LAST
SEEN

WRECK

Whitefish
Pt.

Whitefish
Bay

Sault
Ste. Marie

MICHIGAN'S
UPPER PENINSULA

N
W E
S

MISSING

The True and Tragic Story of
the Disappearance of the
S.S. *Edmund Fitzgerald*

ANDREW KANTAR

Michigan State University Press
East Lansing

All Michigan State University Press Books are produced on paper which meets the requirements of American National Standard of Information Science—Permanence of paper for printed materials ANSI Z 39.48-1984.

Michigan State University Press
East Lansing, Michigan 48823-5202

04 03 02 01   4 5 6 7 8 9

Library of Congress Cataloging-in-Publication Data

Kantar, Andrew Klekner.
   29 missing: the true and tragic story of the disappearance of the
S. S. Edmund Fitzgerald / Andrew Kantar.
      p.   cm.
   Includes bibliographical references.
   Summary: Recounts the sinking of the huge freighter the S. S. Edmund
Fitzgerald in the icy waters of Lake Superior in 1975 and describes subse-
quent expeditions to the wreck site to uncover clues to her mysterious
disappearance.
      ISBN 0-87013-446-9
      1. Edmund Fitzgerald (Ship)—Juvenile literature.   2. Shipwrecks—
Superior, Lake—Juvenile literature.   [1. Edmund Fitzgerald (Ship)
2. Shipwrecks.]   I. Title.
   G530.E26K36   1998
   363.1'23'097749—dc21   98-6350
                                                              CIP
                                                              AC

910.45
6/29/06   KAN   H gift

For Sally, Max, and Emily
Your intellectual energy and natural curiosity
inspire me more than you know.

• Contents •

• Acknowledgements •

An undertaking such as this requires the help and cooperation of many people. I am greatly indebted to them, for without their assistance, this book would not have been possible. Special thanks for the thoughtful commentary provided by maritime expert and author Frederick Stonehouse and to Thomas Farnquist, executive director of the Great Lakes Shipwreck Historical Society and his associate, Sean Ley. Thanks also to Dr. Dianne Monson (University of Minnesota) and Dr. Paul Blake (Ferris State University) for their insights and suggestions. I am appreciative of the photographs I received from Bowling Green State University's Historical Collections of the Great Lakes; C. Patrick Labadie, director of the Lake Superior Maritime Visitor Center of the U.S. Army Corps of Engineers; Linda Richardson of the *Sault Star* (Sault Ste. Marie, Ontario); Harbor Branch Oceanographic Institution; and the Great Lakes Shipwreck Historical Society.

Heartfelt thanks to my father, Dr. Bruce L. Kantar, for his encouragement and wisdom. I am especially grateful to my wife, Fran, who so capably recreated the mapped routes of the *Fitzgerald* and the *Anderson*. She was my most trusted critic, and as always, her love and patience never wavered.

• Preface •

In 1958, when the S.S. *Edmund Fitzgerald* first entered the Great Lakes, she was the biggest ship to sail fresh water in the history of the world. For years, this noble giant not only set shipping records but even shattered her old records. She was the kind of vessel that seamen took pride in. It was an honor to serve on the *Fitzgerald*.

On November 10, 1975, something terrible happened. The *Fitzgerald* and her crew of twenty-nine men were heading across Lake Superior in a snowstorm. The high waves and unrelenting winds battered the ship violently. Eventually she just dropped from sight. There was no call for help, no indication that she was about to sink. Nearby ships could not pick her up on their radar, and attempts at radio contact returned only dead air. How could this 729-foot freighter simply disappear? This is the question that has been asked ever since that stormy night.

Although the ship was finally located at the muddy bottom of Lake Superior, no bodies were ever recovered. The U.S. Coast Guard has officially reported the entire crew as "missing and presumed dead."

Many ships have been lost to the icy depths of Lake Superior, but never before has one so captured the attention of the world. What happened to her? This is the story of the wreck of the *Edmund Fitzgerald*.

·1·

"Graveyard of the Great Lakes"

Few places in this world possess the rugged beauty and natural majesty of the Great Lakes. And few other lakes can stir such terror in the hearts of skilled and experienced sailors. Spanning the border of Canada and the United States, from east to west these are Lakes Ontario, Erie, Huron, Michigan, and Superior.

In all the time that shipping records have been kept, the Great Lakes have claimed more than 6,000 vessels! The largest, deepest, coldest, and, according to some, most frightening and foreboding of these lakes is Lake Superior. Stretching 350 miles, it is the largest body of fresh water in the world. It averages 500 feet deep and is 1,333 feet deep at its deepest spot. It is nearly always cold. Even in summer it reaches only 40 degrees. As late as May you can see the ice just beginning to break up in the harbor in Duluth, Minnesota! Situated atop the north-central United States, Lake Superior is indeed an imposing body of icy fresh water, spanning one Canadian province (Ontario) and three states (Minnesota,

Wisconsin, and Michigan). Superior is so big that one of its islands is a national park—Isle Royale, 44 miles long.

In keeping with its massive size, Superior's mammoth storms are legendary, claiming the lives of hundreds of sailors who have been cast into its numbing depths. The first loss on record was in 1816, a British schooner, ironically named *Invincible*. In all, over five hundred shipwrecks have been documented on Lake Superior, thought by many to be the roughest of the Lakes. Although other lakes lose more ships, they also carry more traffic than Superior. Lake Superior can be dangerous at any time of year, but history has revealed that the month of November can be a particularly perilous time to venture out. In November, cold Arctic air collides with warm southern winds, resulting in early winter storms, when high winds and monster waves rage across all of the Great Lakes.

There is good reason why sailors are in awe of the lake they call "Old Treacherous," especially in November, and it goes beyond superstition and folklore. A good deal has been written, for example, about the November storm of 1913. On that day twelve ships went down, another sixteen washed ashore, and when it was all over, 254 sailors were dead. Six years later, the gales of November raged on November 22, 1919, when the steamer *Myron* sank on Lake Superior off Whitefish Point, Michigan. The only survivor was Captain Walter R. Neal. Amazingly, the following year, eight of the *Myron*'s crew washed ashore at Salt Point— encased in ice! Before the funeral, the horribly contorted, frozen bodies had to be thawed before a roaring fire. The November terror on Lake Superior struck again in 1940, when a frightening storm sank five vessels and killed 67 men. History has shown November to be a cruel and unforgiving time to face the challenge of Lake Superior.

The S.S. *Edmund Fitzgerald*, the last ship to sink in Lake Superior, was also lost in November. By some accounts, the storm of November 10, 1975 was the fiercest ever witnessed on the lake. On this night, the *Edmund Fitzgerald*, a huge ore carrier, went down amid freezing snowy winds and towering waves. There were no witnesses and no survivors. The ship's wreckage still rests at Superior's bottom, over 500 feet below the surface. The shipwreck occurred near Whitefish Point, part of an 80-mile stretch known as the "Graveyard of the Great Lakes" that has claimed 320 sailors' lives. A great deal of mystery has surrounded the *Fitzgerald* tragedy. This is the tale of that terrible voyage.

·2·

The Fitz

O n June 8, 1958, in front of over ten thousand spectators, a gigantic freighter was christened the S.S. *Edmund Fitzgerald* by Mrs. Edmund Fitzgerald, wife of the president of a corporate giant—Northwestern Mutual Insurance Company of Milwaukee. The ship's name seemed appropriate. Edmund was a banker, but he came from a seafaring family. Mr. Fitzgerald's grandfather, John, had skippered several ships on the Great Lakes, as had John's five brothers.

The launching of this great ship was a special event. The *Edmund Fitzgerald*, built by Great Lakes Engineering in River Rouge, Michigan, and owned by the Northwestern Mutual Insurance Company, represented the largest vessel on the Great Lakes, and it remained so until 1971. In fact, at the time of its christening, it was the largest ship ever to enter fresh water. At a staggering 729 feet long she was the length of a towering skyscraper and weighed in at 13,632 tons! This workhorse had engines that could generate 7,000 horsepower, and although it may not seem very fast to us as we drive our cars today, for a freighter she was swift, capable of carrying her heavy loads at a speed of 16 miles per hour. The builders, owners, and crew could not have been more proud of this majestic freighter known as "The Pride of the American Flag." It has been said that the crew was so fond of the *Fitz*, as they called her, that they chased away seagulls from the deck for fear their droppings would disgrace her.

She cost more than eight million dollars to build but proved her worth on many occasions. The *Edmund Fitzgerald* soon acquired a reputation not only as an efficient hauler of iron ore but also as a Great Lakes record setter. The *Fitz* soon held the record for most tons of iron ore hauled in one season, most iron ore carried on one trip, and most tons of ore hauled through the famous and busy Soo Canals, the international passage that connects Lake Superior with Lake Huron. When other ships fell short of her stellar performance, the *Fitz* simply broke her old records and set new ones. When she sailed Lake Superior, it was like a mythological meeting of two giants—one man-made and the other natural. Each was the largest and most powerful force of its kind on earth. Eventually there would be a struggle for supremacy.

Although she was a freighter, an ore carrier, as they are called, the *Edmund Fitzgerald* was equipped with some surprisingly comfortable accommodations. These were reserved for passengers who were special guests aboard this giant of the lakes. For these occasions, the ship was furnished with two plush staterooms that could accommodate four passengers. These guest cabins included tiled baths, plush carpeting, and leather swivel chairs. In addition, there was a luxurious lounge where the guests received excellent service from friendly stewards. At one point during the journey, the Captain would invite the guests to a special candlelight dinner, where uniformed stewards would attend to their needs.

Of course, the accommodations for the crew were not nearly as luxurious, but they were certainly considered adequate for a ship of this type. There were two deckhouses, forward and aft. The forward deckhouse, located toward the front, or bow, of the ship, contained crew accommodations and the pilothouse. The aft deckhouse, located near the rear, or stern, of the ship, provided more crew accommodations as well as the mess room (dining area). The sailors could travel between the two deckhouses by way of port (left side) and starboard (right side) access tunnels that were located below the upper deck. These connecting tunnels were quite a walk, considering that this ship was longer than two football fields!

In case of emergency, the *Edmund Fitzgerald* was equipped with all of the necessary electronic and lifesaving devices. The communication equipment included three separate marine FM radiotelephones. Two of these relied on the ship's power, and, in case of a power loss, the third was powered by rechargeable batteries. In addition, she was equipped with a 100-watt AM radio. In case of a power loss, they also had a 50-watt, battery-powered AM radio.

Interestingly enough, the *Edmund Fitzgerald* had no electronic means by which they could measure lake depth; it had no depth gauge or fathometer. To get these measurements, they had to go through a rather primitive manual process of dropping a knotted line over the vessel's bow (front). A piece of lead was attached to the line's end. The depth was then calculated by simply counting the number of knots in the line after the lead touched the bottom.

Commercial vessels that sail the Great Lakes are required to undergo periodic inspections by the U.S. Coast Guard, and the *Edmund Fitzgerald* was no exception. Of course, lifesaving equipment was inspected, and it was noted that the *Fitzgerald* had two 50-man lifeboats and two 25-man inflatable life rafts. Because the ship had widely separated sleeping quarters (in the forward and aft deckhouses), one raft was situated forward and the other was aft. This way, it was thought, in an emergency all members of the crew would have equal access to the lifesaving equipment. Finally, as required by the Coast Guard, the vessel contained 83 life preservers. Unfortunately, on the terrible night of November 10, none of this lifesaving equipment was used. The entire crew perished. No bodies were ever recovered.

·3·

The Final Journey

n 1975 the *Fitzgerald*, at 17 years of age, was still considered to be relatively young. After all, many ships on the Great Lakes were two or three times her age, and yet the *Fitzgerald* had already made quite a name for herself as a record breaker. Six different times she set and broke the record for a season's haul!

On October 31, just ten days before her final departure of the season, the *Edmund Fitzgerald* underwent a routine upper deck inspection in Toledo, Ohio. The inspectors found some minor cracks to four hatches (openings on the deck that lead to cargo spaces below). The *Fitzgerald* had 21 of these cargo hatches. When viewed from above, these covered hatches looked like a long row of ribs that extended the length of the spar deck (upper deck). Each hatch opening was very large—about as long as those "big rig" trailers you see on the highway. It was not unusual, however, for a busy ship's hatches to show some damage from a season's loading or unloading. Therefore, the inspectors allowed the

Fitzgerald to venture out on November 9 with the operators' promise to make the repairs during the winter off season. This was not the first time that the Fitzgerald had required repairs for accidental and routine damage. All Great Lakes freighters suffer a fair amount of damage.

On November 8, the day before their scheduled departure, the National Weather Service reported "a typical November storm" over the Oklahoma Panhandle that was moving northeast. The next day, November 9, was a warm, brilliantly sunny autumn day in Superior, Wisconsin, where the *Fitzgerald* was awaiting the season's last run. At about 8:30 that morning, "*Big Fitz*" was loaded up with over 26,000 tons of taconite pellets—about as heavy as 17,300 cars! Taconite pellets are little balls of processed iron ore. They are a valuable material in making steel that is used to make cars. That is why their final destination was 700 miles away in Detroit, the home of the world's leading car manufacturers. The round trip was expected to take about five days.

As the captain and crew of the *Fitz* made final preparations for her 2:15 P.M. departure, they did not suspect that soon they would be on a collision course with one of the worst storms in recent history on the Great Lakes. The 29-man crew was an experienced group of sailors, ranging in age from their twenties to their sixties. Most were forty or older. Mainly, they came from Ohio (13) and Wisconsin (8); the remaining eight were from Minnesota (3); Florida (2); and Michigan, Pennsylvania, and California (1).

The only crew change was a last-minute decision based on a doctor's exam of Dick Bishop, the ship's steward (cook). On November 8, the day before they were to ship out, a doctor ordered Dick to stay behind because of serious stomach troubles—bleeding ulcers. Dick, 28 years old, was very disappointed about missing this last run of the season. Strange though it may seem, this may be the only time in history that a case of bleeding ulcers actually *saved* someone's life. Bishop was ably replaced by Robert Rafferty, a 62-year-old grandfather who had logged 44 years at sea. Known for his baking skills, Rafferty loved the *Fitz* and its large kitchen, so when given another opportunity to sail on it, he jumped at the chance.

The skipper of this grand and majestic vessel was Captain Ernest McSorley, a master seaman with 44 years of experience. His long and distinguished career began at the age of 18 as a deckhand. He moved rapidly through the ranks and in 1950 became the youngest captain on the Great Lakes. From the time of its christening, in 1958, it had always been his dream to be captain of the *Fitzgerald*. *"Big Fitz"* was the flagship, the best of Columbia Transportation Division's fleet of twenty freighters, which were operated by Oglebay Norton Company of Cleveland. In Great Lakes shipping, it was generally understood that the best ships were entrusted to the most worthy captains. In 1971, McSorley replaced Captain Peter Pulcer, who retired. When McSorley was selected to captain the *Fitz*, it established him as one of the best skippers on the Great Lakes. As captain, he would typically spend nine to ten months each year on board. As he was about to embark on this last journey of the season, and after many years of memorable adventures on the Great Lakes, Captain McSorley now had his eye on retirement.

At 2:15 P.M., after an uneventful, routine loading, the *Fitz* departed, traveling at what was for her a pretty good speed of 16 mph. Two hours later, at 4:30 P.M., near Two Harbors, Minnesota, the *Fitz* sighted the U.S. Steel Corporation's *Arthur M. Anderson*, another huge freighter with a load of taconite pellets. Both vessels proceeded eastward, about ten to twenty miles apart, with the *Fitz* in the lead. The *Anderson*, skippered by Captain Jessie "Bernie" Cooper, was headed for Gary, Indiana. Together, these two ships would endure the same terrible storm of November 10, but only one of them would survive.

·4·

The Storm Worsens

Later that afternoon, as the *Fitz* and the *Anderson* lumbered at a slow but determined pace across Lake Superior, the Oklahoma storm began to build, moving north through Kansas and east over Iowa and then Wisconsin. As the storm front made its way toward Michigan's Upper Peninsula and Lake Superior, the National Weather Service (NWS) began to realize that this might not be just another storm. By 7:00 P.M., gale warnings were issued for all of Lake Superior. The new forecast for eastern Lake Superior warned of winds of nearly 45 miles per hour (38 knots) and waves up to 10 feet.

By 1:00 the next morning, on Monday, November 10, the *Fitz* was about 20 miles south of Isle Royale. Unrelenting heavy rains limited the captain's visibility. Gale-force winds were clocked at 60 mph (52 knots), and ten-foot waves repeatedly pummeled the mighty vessel. The danger of being accidentally blown overboard into the wild water, a chilling 37°F, was enough to keep the crew alert at all times.

One hour later, at 2:00 A.M., Captain Cooper of the *Anderson* contacted Captain McSorley by radiotelephone. Both were concerned about the threatening weather. Cooper noted that the gale warnings of 7:00 P.M. were now storm warnings. The sailors knew that the storm was building into something more serious and more dangerous by the hour. The NWS was predicting winds of nearly 60 mph and 15-foot waves.

Knowing what high winds could do to ships sailing Superior's southern shore, both skippers agreed to change their route. Rather than following the much shorter but more dangerous southern shore, they took the longer, safer northeasterly passage, following the more protected Canadian shore. With the swifter *Fitz* leading the way, they would sail a course between Michigan's Keeweenaw Peninsula and Isle Royale. Experienced sailors on Superior have traditionally done this in bad weather. It is better to take a little longer and be safe.

Throughout the lonely night, the two giant freighters made steady progress, despite treacherous 50-mph winds and the constant struggle with increasingly large waves. Considering everything, it was fairly smooth sailing as the two ships headed eastward.

As the freighters journeyed across the stormy lake, people on Michigan's Upper Peninsula (U.P.) began to awaken at 7:00 A.M. It seemed like another one of those cold, wet November days. It was the kind of day that people living on the Great Lakes see as a sign that winter is approaching. Sleepy-eyed parents and children still in their pajamas wandered into the kitchen and ate some warm breakfast. The heavy winds rattled the windows and whistled through the cracks in the front door, prompting some kids to ask, "Hey, are we going to school today?" As soon as they turned on their radios and television sets, they heard reports of a storm that was gathering momentum and blowing hard over the U.P. Today schools would be closed, trees would be ripped from the soil, windows would explode with the force of the winds, and many homes would be without power. November 10 was not just another autumn storm. This day would become legend.

Just as the residents of the U.P. were awakening to the pounding winds, the *Fitz* made a routine morning radio report to their company office at 7:20 A.M. They said that because of the fierce weather and the early-morning decision to change their course, they might be a little late coming into the Soo Locks (Sault St. Marie, Michigan).

By early afternoon, the storm center had crossed Lake Superior to the west of Michipicoten Island—right where the *Fitz* was. Now past Isle Royale and the Keeweenaw Peninsula, the *Fitz* was only about 11 miles off the coast of Michipicoten Island. She had successfully navigated the "northern" route that had been planned with the *Anderson*. As the *Fitz* approached Michipicoten Island (to the north) and Caribou Island (to the south), it was time to plot a new course. They would pass *between* the two islands. With the *Fitz* in the lead and the *Anderson* about nine miles behind, the ships planned to sail just below Michipicoten Island and above Caribou Island. After clearing the islands, they would sail southeast to Whitefish Bay. Navigating this route under these hazardous conditions presented some serious concerns. They were about to enter the perilous "Graveyard of the Great Lakes."

At 1:40 P.M., after clearing Michipicoten, McSorley radioed Cooper and reported that his vessel was "rolling some." Cooper then informed McSorley that he was changing his course slightly so that he, too, would clear Michipicoten. Cooper expected a wind shift and wanted the *Anderson* to take the big waves from the stern (rear).

About ten minutes after the captains spoke, the winds slowed down to a gentle six mph. This did not last long, however, for less than an hour later (2:45 P.M.), the *Fitz* was again weathering winds of nearly 50 mph. It had started to snow heavily, and the frenzied sea lashed angrily at the *Fitz*. Although the *Anderson* could still follow the *Fitz* electronically on her radar, she now lost sight of the proud giant. The *Fitz* would never physically be *seen* again.

·5·

"I've Never Seen Anything Like It In My Life"

At 3:20 P.M., the *Anderson* approached Michipicoten Island. It was snowing, 50-mph winds whipped across the lake, and twelve- to sixteen-foot waves washed up over her deck. The crew in the *Anderson*'s pilothouse observed the path of the *Fitz* on radar. The *Fitz*, with a 16-mile lead, was attempting to navigate a northeast course past Caribou Island's dangerous Six-Fathom Shoal, a relatively shallow area just off the island. A fathom is six-feet deep, and a shoal is simply a shallow area. For most of us, six fathoms, or 36 feet, is deep water. But this is a shallow spot in Lake Superior, where the average depth is 500 feet! This would be especially dangerous for large freighters. Freighter captains knew that the risk of shoaling (doing damage by hitting bottom in a shallow spot) made Six-Fathom Shoal an extremely hazardous stretch, especially in rough water that forced the cargo giants to pitch up and down. Knowing they would be next to encounter Six-Fathom Shoal, the *Anderson*'s captain and first mate watched their radar with concern as the *Fitz* tried to avoid the shoal.

Experienced sailors knew that it was absolutely necessary to steer wide of this spot. If a big freighter hit the rocky bottom, there was no telling what damage the ship's hull would suffer or how long she could stay afloat, especially in a storm like this. The big *Fitz* was being violently bounced and rolled on the monster sea as she attempted to clear the shoal. Captain Cooper of the *Anderson* watched intently as the *Fitz*'s radar image drifted slowly on the screen, nearing the shoal. Right then he knew that she had come a little too close! Clearly, the screaming winds and blowing snow had made it difficult and hazardous to navigate. The *Fitz* had made it past the shoal, but what damage had she suffered in the process? Cooper saw what the force of the storm had done to the *Fitz*'s course, and he knew that the *Anderson* would have to clear Six-Fathom Shoal by a greater distance.

Ten minutes later, Cooper received a call from the *Fitz*. Captain McSorley reported a fence rail down and two vents that had been lost or damaged and were taking in water. McSorley said that he had two pumps going to control the flooding from the lost vents. He also said his ship had a "list" (was leaning a little to one side). Although this was not viewed as an emergency call for help, McSorley was concerned enough to slow his ship down and request that the *Anderson* follow them. The *Fitz* was now 17 miles ahead, and visibility was poor due to falling snow. The *Anderson* had lost sight of the *Fitz* but continued to track her on radar. Judging by the type of problems they had reported and the tone of Captain McSorley's message, the *Anderson* did not feel that the *Fitz* or her crew were in any immediate danger.

What were they thinking, aboard the *Fitz* at this time? By now, Captain McSorley and his First Mate John McCarthy, a fellow Ohioan, were probably concerned about possible damage to the ship. It is likely they knew they had come too close to Six-Fathom Shoal. If so, they might have banged the ship's hull on the rocky bottom. Was she taking in water from the external damage to the hull? There was no way to know just how much damage she could have suffered. In addition, they had the lost vents to think about. Water was seeping in there, too, but at least they had their pumps working on that problem.

Should they try to turn around and make a rough landing on Caribou Island? In a raging sea such as this they would run the risk of capsizing. What about lowering the crew into lifeboats or life rafts? Imagine trying to survive 16-foot waves and 50-mph winds in a lifeboat or an inflatable raft! It would be like trying to survive an avalanche of snow on a sled. If the giant waves washed across the deck of the mighty *Fitz*, what chance would a lifeboat have? They would never be able to stay afloat long enough for the *Anderson* to come and pick them up. Besides, the huge *Anderson* would be no more adept at maneuvering in this storm than the *Fitz*. McSorley and McCarthy were experienced seamen. They knew that their only hope for survival was to try with all their might to push into Whitefish Bay, push as though their very lives depended on it.

About the time that the *Fitz* was struggling past the shoal (3:30–4:00 P.M.), the Coast Guard issued an emergency warning for all ships on Lake Superior to find a safe place and drop anchor. For the *Fitz*, however, there was no such place. By now the storm was in full force, with the Soo Locks reporting wind gusts up to 96 mph! The Mackinac Bridge, the 5-mile suspension bridge that separates Lake Michigan and Lake Huron, was swaying violently in 85-mph winds.

Then, at about 4:10 P.M., First Mate Morgan Clark of the *Anderson* received some chilling news from the *Fitz*. She had lost her radars—even the backup system. When there is poor visibility, radar serves as the ship's eyes. No radar, combined with blowing snow and fierce winds, made the *Fitz* virtually blind in this storm. Pitching and rolling, she was open to assault on every side by the crashing waves and heaving sea. Because of the storm and the rapidly approaching darkness, it would be easy to become disoriented and confused. The *Fitz*, therefore, asked the *Anderson* for help in navigating her to Whitefish Bay and safety. The *Anderson* agreed to serve as the "eyes" of the *Fitz*, advising her of oncoming or passing vessels.

Shortly after reporting the loss of her radar, the *Fitz* sent out a radio call to "any vessel near Whitefish Point." Captain Cedric

C. Woodard of the Swedish freighter *Avafors* responded. He was leaving Whitefish Point bound for Duluth, Minnesota. McSorley asked if the lighthouse on Whitefish Point was functioning and if the radio beacon was operating. Woodard could see the tower but observed that the light was out and said that he could not pick up the radio beacon. At about 4:40 P.M., McSorley then tried to confirm Woodard's observation with a call to the Coast Guard at Grand Marais. Grand Marais then contacted the Coast Guard at Sault St. Marie. The word was official: *There was no light due to a power failure, and the Whitefish radio beacon was not operating.* There was no light and no radio signal. Without her radar and awash with massive waves, the *Fitz* was struggling mightily for survival against 68-mph winds and the battering sea.

Captain Woodard of the *Avafors* put in a call at 5:15 P.M. to the *Fitz* with some good news to report. The power had been restored to the Whitefish Point Lighthouse; however, the radio beacon was still dead. He then told McSorley that the upbound *Avafors* was about to leave Whitefish Point behind and wanted to know about the "conditions out there." Captain McSorley reported winds of sixty to seventy mph and 30-foot waves! He added that his radar was completely out, that they were taking in lots of water, and that his ship was now leaning badly. At one point, Woodard overheard McSorley shout to someone, "Don't allow nobody on deck!" Just before signing off, McSorley's voice penetrated the stormy darkness with these ominous words: "Big sea—I've never seen anything like it in my life."

Figure 1. The S.S. *Edmund Fitzgerald:* The "Pride of the American Flag."
Photograph by Peter Vander Linden, courtesy of the U.S. Army Corps of Engineers.

Figure 2. The record-setting *Fitz* on another run.

Courtesy of the Historical Collections of the Great Lakes at Bowling Green State University.

Figure 3. The *Fitzgerald* fully loaded.
Courtesy of the Historical Collections of the Great Lakes at
Bowling Green State University.

Figure 4. A car is dwarfed next to the giant *Arthur M. Anderson*.
Photograph by Ken Thro, courtesy of the U.S. Army Corps of Engineers.

Figure 5. A view of the *Anderson's* stern as she plows through broken ice.
Photograph by H. G. Weis, courtesy of the U.S. Army Corps of Engineers.

Figure 6. The *Fitzgerald's* bent and battered No. 2 lifeboat speaks silently of the lake's violence on that terrible night. In the foreground are life jackets that were never used.
Courtesy of *The Sault Star,* Sault Ste. Marie, Ontario.

Figure 7. An unused inflatable life raft from the *Fitzgerald* that was recovered in the search following the freighter's mysterious disappearance.

Courtesy of *The Sault Star*, Sault Ste. Marie, Ontario.

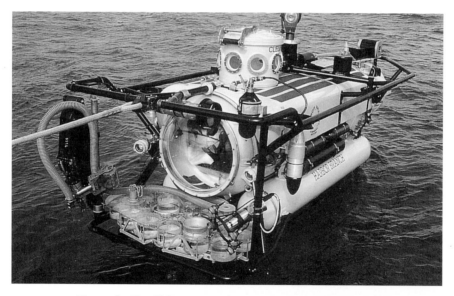

Figure 8. The *Clelia*, a minisubmarine, was taken down to the wreck site of the *Fitzgerald* in 1994.

Photograph is courtesy of the Harbor Branch Oceanographic Institution.

Figure 9. The *Fitzgerald's* pilothouse door, viewed from the *Clelia's* large dome (1994).
Photograph by Jene Quirin, courtesy of the Great Lakes Shipwreck Historical Society.

Figure 10. A view of the *Fitzgerald's* crow's nest and radar mast from a depth of more than four-hundred feet. The "C" stands for Columbia Transportation Company. Amazingly, the light bulbs outlining the "C" were unbroken.
Photograph by Tom Farnquist, courtesy of the Great Lakes Shipwreck Historical Society.

Figure 11. NEWTSUIT diver Bruce Fuoco prepares to recover the
Fitzgerald's bell (1995).
Photograph by Jene Quirin, courtesy of the Great Lakes Shipwreck
Historical Society.

Figure 12. The NEWTSUIT diver is lowered into Lake
Superior's chilling waters (1995).

Photograph by Jene Quirin, courtesy of the Great Lakes
Shipwreck Historical Society.

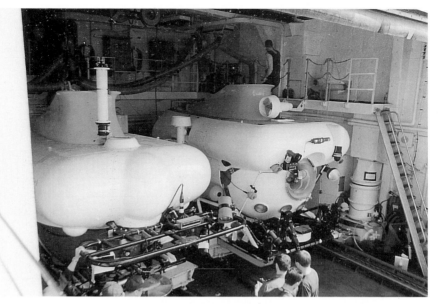

Figure 13. Canadian Navy's submersibles, *Pisces IV* (left) and *SDL-1*, used in the 1995 bell recovery mission.

Photograph by Tom Farnquist, courtesy of the Great Lakes Shipwreck Historical Society.

Figure 14. *SDL-1* on its way down to the wreck site (1995).

Photograph by Tom Farnquist, courtesy of the Great Lakes Shipwreck Historical Society.

·6·

Vanished!

A t 6:00 P.M. the *Anderson*, ten to fifteen miles behind the *Fitz*, reported the same high seas that Captain McSorley had described to Captain Woodard about 45 minutes earlier. Captain Cooper attempted to steer the *Anderson* on a steady course despite 25-foot waves and 65- to 70-mph winds. Time and again the waves crashed down upon her slippery deck. Fortunately, she had successfully cleared the Six-Fathom Shoal and was now 15 miles past Caribou Island. Although they had all they could do to maintain their position, the *Anderson* knew that the *Fitz* needed her radar guidance. They tried to keep a careful watch and noticed that the *Fitz* was apparently drifting to the left.

An hour later, amid rain and snow, the unrelenting winds (reported at 57 mph) continued to bear down upon the *Anderson*. Winds in the vicinity were reported as gusting up to 75 mph (65 knots)! At about 7:10 P.M., with the *Fitz* about 10 miles ahead and 15 miles off of Crisp Point, the *Anderson*'s first mate, Morgan Clark, radioed in to warn her of an oncoming "target" that appeared on the radar. The *Fitz*, without radar and blinded by the storm, asked, "Well, am I going to clear?" Clark replied, "Yes, he is going to pass to the west of you." The *Fitz* responded, "Well, fine."

After this brief exchange, Morgan Clark, knowing that the *Fitz* had been taking in some water due to the lost vents, asked, "Oh, by the way, how are you making out with your problem?" The *Fitz* replied, "We are holding our own." Clark said, "Okay, fine, I will be talking to you later." Unfortunately this was not to be, for just after those seemingly reassuring words, the *Fitz* was never heard from again. All radio contact was lost. The *Fitz* dropped off the *Anderson*'s radar screen. A 729-foot ship and her entire crew of twenty-nine had simply disappeared!

Ten minutes later, the *Anderson* observed on its radar three outgoing saltwater ships about seventeen miles away—the *Nanfri*, *Benfri*, and *Avafors*. Cooper was sure that the *Fitz*, which was supposed to be much closer than these ships, just had to be somewhere on the radar screen. Yet she was nowhere to be seen. Where were her lights? Could she have had a blackout? The *Anderson*'s Captain Cooper and First Mate Clark were disturbed and perplexed by the sudden disappearance. Cooper ordered everyone on the bridge to look for a silhouette on the horizon—anything that could possibly be the *Fitz*. But no matter how they tried to locate her, there was no escaping it—no radar, no lights, no radio contact. Just 17 miles from the safe anchorage of Whitefish Point, the *Edmund Fitzgerald* had vanished!

An increasingly anxious Cooper repeatedly tried to make radio contact with the *Fitz*. Then, thinking that a radio malfunction might be the problem, Cooper tried making contact with the *William Clay Ford* at Whitefish Point. The radio call went through without a hitch, proving there was no malfunction. The *Ford* said that the *Anderson* came in "loud and clear," yet neither the *Ford* nor the *Anderson* could detect the *Fitzgerald* on radar.

After adjusting their radar, the *Anderson* could still pick up only three ships—there was no sign of the *Fitz*. A worried Captain Cooper radioed the U.S. Coast Guard on its emergency frequency and expressed his concerns about losing the *Fitz* on radar. He then contacted the passing vessels, but none had seen her. How could the "Queen of the Lakes" drop out of sight so quickly? They reported that they were holding their own, and then within minutes they vanished from the radar. There was no call for help, no "Mayday," and no indication they were sinking. It just did not make sense.

At 8:00 P.M., Captain Albert Jacovetti of the *Nanfri* reported to Cooper that he could pick up the *Anderson* on radar, but like all the others, they could not find the *Fitz*. A half hour later, in a second alert to the Coast Guard at Sault Saint Marie, Cooper revealed his worst fears:

> I am very concerned with the welfare of the steamer *Edmund Fitzgerald*. He was right in front of us experiencing a little difficulty. He was taking on a small amount of water and none of the upbound ships have passed him. I can see no lights as before, and I don't have him on radar. I just hope he didn't take a nose dive!

After finally reaching Whitefish Point at about 9:00 P.M., the *Anderson* logged winds that were still howling at 55 mph. If the *Fitzgerald* had made just 17 more miles, she would have survived. Instead, the thrashing sea unceremoniously dragged the "Pride of the American Flag" and her entire crew more than 500 feet below to her icy depths. That night on Lake Superior, the end came swiftly.

·7·

The Search Begins

ust after Captain Cooper's second call to the Coast Guard station at about 8:30 P.M., the Coast Guard sent out a radio call to the *Fitzgerald*. At this time, the Coast Guard even asked for help from a nearby commercial radio station in Rogers City, Michigan. Neither signal received a response from the lost giant.

Soon after the radio attempts failed, between 10:00 and 11:00 P.M., the Coast Guard dispatched one plane (an HU–16) and two helicopters (HH–52). Braving high winds and poor visibility, the search plane made it to the *Fitz*'s last-known location just before 11:00 P.M. By 1:00 A.M., all three, the aircraft and two helicopters, were on the scene, enduring 70-mph winds. One of the helicopters was equipped with the powerful Night Sun, a remote-control searchlight that generates 3.8 million candlepower. Together, this search and rescue air team scanned the rolling seas in an effort to find any evidence of the *Fitzgerald*. The search had begun.

In addition to the air search, two Coast Guard cutters, the *Naugatuck* and the *Woodrush*, were ordered out to coordinate support on the water. Unfortunately, the *Naugatuck* had mechanical problems and could not make it out until the next afternoon, and the *Woodrush*, based in Duluth, Minnesota, was over 300 miles from the scene. One 40-foot patrol boat was, however, sent out on the morning of November 11 and searched until late afternoon. All other Coast Guard vessels were either undergoing repairs or too far away to be of immediate help.

Because of the lack of search and rescue support on the water, the Coast Guard put in an urgent request for assistance from any commercial vessels anchored in the area of Whitefish Bay. That night there were seven American and Canadian vessels anchored in the vicinity. All were contacted by the Coast Guard to aid in the search. However, the high winds and dangerous conditions convinced all but two of them to remain in the safe harbor. At 9:00 P.M., just after surviving the terrible seas, the *Anderson* was asked to turn around and go back out. The captain agreed and by 2:00 A.M., at great risk, the *Anderson* again braved the fierce winds and fought the high water, desperately searching for any sign of the lost giant. Throughout the night and well into the next day, the *William Clay Ford* joined the *Anderson* in its search for the lost *Fitzgerald*. A Canadian vessel, the *Hilda Marjanne*, also responded to the Coast Guard's request, but the violent weather forced her to abandon the effort, and she turned back after only 30 minutes.

Earlier in the evening, at about the time the *Fitz* disappeared from the *Anderson*'s radar screen, three outgoing international saltwater vessels were observed—the *Nanfri*, *Benfri*, and *Avafors*. At the time of the search, these vessels also were contacted by the Coast Guard. The seas, however, were too rough, and reversing a course under these conditions could have caused the ships to capsize.

By dawn on November 11, the air search team had expanded to four planes and two helicopters. In addition to the first three aircraft on the scene—the Coast Guard's plane and two helicopters—there were now three C–130 planes (a Michigan Air

National Guard plane, a Canadian plane, and a Coast Guard plane from North Carolina).

Between November 11 and November 13, additional air and water support was provided by the Canadian Coast Guard, and all twelve vessels that were anchored at or near Whitefish Point now participated in the search. The Coast Guard cutters *Naugatuck* and *Woodrush*, had also now made it to the scene. However, despite these search and rescue efforts, there was still no sign of the ship that so mysteriously vanished.

It was not until November 14, when a Navy aircraft became involved, that a location was pinpointed for the sunken *Fitzgerald.* This plane carried a piece of equipment that could detect magnetic fields (Magnetic Anamoly Detection or MAD). It was hoped that the metal hull of the *Fitzgerald* could be located this way, even as far down as the muddy depths of Lake Superior. Sure enough, a strong magnetic pull was picked up about seventeen miles off of Whitefish Point. At this spot, there was also an oil slick. Although there was no physical evidence of the ship, six months later it was learned that this was the very place where the *Fitzgerald* lost its struggle with the sea.

The initial search, following the *Fitzgerald*'s disappearance, yielded very little. No bodies were found. There were no witnesses to the tragedy. The ship went down virtually without a trace. The remnants that bobbed to the surface, miles away, were pitifully few. A little past 8:00 A.M. on November 11, the *Anderson* located a portion of one of the *Fitzgerald*'s two lifeboats. It was drifting peacefully about nine miles east of where the *Fitzgerald* went down. Then, only an hour later, the *Anderson* spotted the second lifeboat. The Coast Guard investigation stated that the two boats were "severely damaged," and noted that portions of the metal wreckage were "twisted and distorted." Clearly, these inanimate "survivors" had been through a violent ordeal.

That same morning, shortly after the sighting of the second lifeboat, one of the *Fitzgerald*'s 25-man inflatable life rafts was seen floating upright. It was recovered by the freighter *Roger Blough* and contained things like flashlight batteries, paddles, and a repair kit to patch any tears in the raft. Later that day, the *Fitzgerald's* other life raft was picked up on the shore by the Provincial Police of Ontario, Canada.

What might have happened if the *Fitzgerald's* crew had some-how managed to escape into the lifeboats or life rafts? After all, these life vessels survived. Survival for the men, however, would still have been unlikely under the conditions that prevailed on the night of November 10. One of the greatest threats, and a deadly killer on Superior, is hypothermia. Hypothermia occurs when, after being immersed in icy water, the human body temperature drops dangerously low. If untreated, it eventually leads to death. Remember, that night Lake Superior's waters were a bone-chilling 37°F. Under these conditions, it would probably have taken less than five minutes for hypothermia to take hold. Also, on that evening the icy waves were twenty-five to thirty feet high and the winds gusted to 70 miles per hour. The wall of water was capable of sinking a 729-foot freighter. What chance would men in a lifeboat have had under these circumstances? Furthermore, the lifeboats and inflatable life rafts would have required time to unload from the ship and to allow the crew to enter. Time was one thing the crew of the *Fitzgerald* did not have. Something brought her down so quickly there was not even time for an SOS or a dis-tress signal. One moment they radioed in, "We're holding our own," and the next they were simply gone—without a word.

Besides the lifeboats and inflatable life rafts, the Coast Guard investigation revealed that the search parties located twenty life preservers or pieces of preservers, eight oars or pieces of oars, thirteen life rings with pieces of line attached, a stepladder, a bro-ken extension ladder, a wooden stool, various pieces of scrap wood, and other odds and ends. No personal effects of the crew were found.

The November search for the *Fitzgerald's* sunken hull con-cluded with two sonar searches that probed the depths of Lake Superior in the area that registered a strong magnetic field. These sonar scans use sound to determine the location, depth, and approximate size of objects that lie beneath the surface. The first sonar scan was conducted between November 14 and November 16. Amazingly, it revealed two very large objects (each about 300 feet long) at the bottom of the lake. Despite strong winds and treacherous lake conditions, a second scan was ordered about one week later, and it confirmed the first scan's findings. Although these sonar scans were not physical proof that the *Fitzgerald* was that giant object lying 530 feet beneath them, it was assumed that her valiant effort and tragic voyage ended here.

Despite the strong evidence that magnetic detection and sonar scanning equipment offered, visual proof was still needed. Were these massive pieces of metal actually the *Fitzgerald*, or could they be remnants of some other vessel that met a similar fate, years earlier? To answer this question, in May 1976, almost six months after the November searches had ended, a fascinating new piece of technology was introduced into the investigation. The Coast Guard enlisted the help of a U.S. Navy system called the Cable-controlled Underwater Recovery Vehicle or CURV III, for short. It was hoped that, if lake conditions were favorable, this remarkable vehicle would be their underwater eyes. They were about to get their first glimpse of the *Fitzgerald.*

The compact CURV III was a mobile underwater unit, equipped with two black-and-white television cameras, a 35mm camera, lights, and a special arm that could be manipulated. It was sort of like a robot with cameras. Because of these cameras, CURV III operators could observe everything on television screens and videotape. The CURV III was capable of going down 7,000 feet—much deeper than Lake Superior's deepest point. It was electrically powered and operated from a control center aboard the support ship.

Between May 20 and May 28, the CURV III made twelve dives and was on the bottom of Lake Superior for a total of 56 hours. During this time, the Coast Guard was able to "see," for the first time, the sunken *Fitzgerald*! The missing ship had finally been located. The CURV III's hours on the lake's bottom were well spent. The Coast Guard now had plenty of visual evidence of the *Fitzgerald*—over 43,000 feet of videotape and almost 900 color photographs.

Now that the location had been verified, the Coast Guard could observe, firsthand, how the *Fitzgerald* had broken up. Resting in Canadian waters just north of the International Boundary, the wreckage was found in two huge pieces, along with scattered metal from the disintegrated middle section. One part, the ship's bow (front end), was lying upright and measured 276 feet long. The stern (rear end) was upside down and measured 253 feet. On both the bow and stern sections, the name S.S. *Edmund Fitzgerald* was clearly printed. Between these two massive chunks of sunken metal the Coast Guard reported finding a lot of "distorted metal . . . over a distance of some 200 feet," like the remnants of a huge explosion. That is exactly what some experts believe happened to the *Fitz*—she actually propelled herself directly to bottom and exploded on impact. With tons of metal scattered over about three acres of lake bottom, it is no wonder that the sonar and magnetic detection equipment alerted the searchers to this location.

The underwater survey revealed that mounds of mud covered all of the ship's wreckage. In fact, every time the CURV III moved around the sunken vessel, clouds of mud rose, making it quite difficult to get clear pictures or even to see the wreckage. Throughout the many hours that the CURV III crawled upon the lake's murky bottom, circling the lost ship, no bodies were ever seen. The ship had been found, but the men were still missing and presumed dead.

·8·

Why Did The *Fitzgerald* Sink?

Now that the *Fitzgerald* had been located, an investigation was planned to determine why and how a ship of this size could sink so quickly. What went wrong? Could it have been prevented? Was anyone at fault? The U.S. Coast Guard Marine Board of Investigation set out to find the answers to these questions.

Because there were no survivors or witnesses to the tragedy, the investigation team had to rely on many other sources of information. Several people testified to the committee. These included seamen who had at one time served on the *Fitzgerald*, crew members of ships that were nearby at the time of the disappearance, employees of the company that owned the *Fitzgerald*, Coast Guardsmen and others who participated in the search, and personnel from the National Weather Service. In addition, the investigators carefully examined the CURV's underwater survey of the wreckage and the debris recovered from the search and rescue operation.

One thing became quite clear. Although the *Fitzgerald* had reported problems along the way, none was serious enough to have caused the ship to go down. The loss of two vents and a broken fence rail would not have sunk this mighty ship. Besides, McSorley had said that he had two pumps working to relieve the flooding brought on by the problem with the vents. Something else must have happened, something of which the captain was not aware. But what?

The Coast Guard investigators knew that, without any survivors, they could only speculate as to what had caused the *Fitzgerald* to sink. They concluded that, most probably, the *Fitzgerald* could no longer maintain its balance and float because of a huge amount of flooding in the cargo hold.

How did the water make its way into the cargo hold? To understand this, you have to realize that the hatches on the top deck (spar deck) lead to the cargo areas. If enough water seeps in through the hatches, a ship could lose its ability to float. Such flooding could cause the ship to lean far to one side (giving it a "list," as McSorley had reported). In the case of the *Fitzgerald*, the major problem was not the intake of water from the loss of two vents but rather the massive flooding in the cargo area, water that probably came in through the ship's hatches. As the *Fitzgerald* took in more and more water, she became less stable. By the time she "dove into a wall of water," she was no longer able to float and went down almost instantly—nose first. Imagine a ship, over 700-feet long, diving nose down in 530 feet of water. When she hit bottom, a good 200 feet of her stern could well have still been poking out of the water! Because she plunged so suddenly and because the pilot house was at the ship's front, there was no way to send out a call for help. According to the Coast Guard, the *Fitzgerald* literally broke up on impact with the lake's bottom. The crew was trapped. They were pulled underwater before they could even attempt to free up any lifeboats or rafts. According to some, many of the crew may have remained alive in a sealed section of the stern for several horrifying minutes after the ship hit bottom and shattered. It is widely believed that most of the bodies of the doomed crew still remain sealed within the ship's stern. Some say that the *Fitz* blew apart when she hit bottom, since much of the middle section or cargo area is missing in the wreckage.

The investigators noticed that while Captain McSorley had reported certain damage to his ship, he had never indicated what might have caused it. They struggled with this question. The Marine Board wondered what could have caused external damage serious enough that it would lead to massive flooding. Their investigation led them primarily to two possibilities. The first, and perhaps most likely, was that the *Fitzgerald* had struck an unidentified floating object. This object would have then been thrown aboard in the heavy seas, causing damage to the topside. According to the time plan, this could have occurred about the time the ship encountered the snowstorm and lost its radar. Without the radar, the floating object would have been difficult to detect and the storm would have made it difficult to see.

Shoaling (scraping bottom in a shallow area) near Caribou Island was considered the other possible cause of the flooding. If this had happened, damage either above or below the waterline could have allowed water to enter through the ship's hull. You will recall that Captain Cooper of the *Anderson* feared that the *Fitzgerald* had come a little too close to the Six-Fathom Shoal. While the Marine Board did not believe that shoaling was as likely as the collision with a floating object, they admitted that a "light grounding" was a distinct possibility.

In 1978, about one year after the Coast Guard Marine Board investigation, the National Transportation Safety Board (NTSB) conducted its own study to determine the cause of the *Fitzgerald's* sinking. Both groups agreed that the hatch openings allowed massive amounts of water to flow into the cargo hold, causing the ship to lean, lose its buoyancy, and eventually sink. The NTSB findings, however, differed from the Coast Guard's in that they thought the hatch covers had actually collapsed, causing rapid and sudden flooding. The Coast Guard, on the other hand, thought the flooding, caused by "ineffective hatch closures," had occurred gradually and, therefore, had gone undetected. By the time the cargo area became sufficiently flooded to affect the ship's ability to float, it was too late to do anything.

Like the Coast Guard, the NTSB assigned the same possible causes for the massive flooding. Most of the investigators believed in the leaking cargo hatch theory, while a minority supported the shoaling theory.

In addition to the two main theories, however, there is yet another explanation offered for the *Fitzgerald*'s sudden disappearance. Some seamen believe that a large wave phenomenon known as the "Three Sisters" was responsible for the tragedy on that November evening. The "Three Sisters," or three big seas, as it is sometimes called, is not just a colorful bit of sea lore. It is an actual scientific phenomenon involving three giant waves that occur in rapid succession. The pummeling of these waves on a ship's deck can lead to tragic consequences. When this happens, one wave hits, then another follows, and another—sometimes covering the entire deck. The three massive waves do not give a ship time to recover. The Three Sisters can, therefore, be very treacherous in a big storm. Those who believe the Three Sisters theory estimate that only ten seconds elapsed between each of the three waves in the attack. If this had happened, these three waves would have dumped 10 million pounds of water on her forward deck and remained there for a full twenty seconds! This extra water weight, coupled with a cargo of 52 million pounds and the flooding that had already taken place, would have been enough to tip the nose downward so that the decks were practically submerged. From there, the *Fitzgerald* could have continued its descent through Superior's great depths until it hit bottom.

Which theory is correct? No one knows for sure. It is all part of the mystery surrounding the tragic loss of this magnificent vessel and her crew. In their investigations, neither the Coast Guard Marine Board nor the National Transportation Safety Board suggested that Captain McSorley was in any way to blame for the tragedy. The investigative teams agreed that he and his crew did everything they could to survive the violently slashing waters.

·9·

The *Fitz* Revisited: Exploring The Wreckage

lthough the explanation of its sinking remains a mystery to this day, since the *Fitz* was lost, there have been some intriguing explorations of the wreckage site. On September 24, 1980, two divers from Jacques Cousteau's famous ship, *Calypso*, took a submarine down for about thirty minutes, initiating the first manned dive to examine the *Fitzgerald*'s remains. The *Calypso* is well known for its worldwide undersea explorations. The findings of this team, led by Jacques' son, Jean-Michel, supported the earlier Coast Guard report. However, based on the *Fitzgerald*'s damage, they concluded that she broke up on the lake's surface before sinking. The Coast Guard report, on the other hand, maintained that the ship's hull had split when she hit bottom: "[the ship's] bow pitched down . . . the cargo rushed forward, the bow plowed into the bottom of the lake," and the ship's middle then "disintegrated."

Yet another look at the *Fitzgerald* took place during an expedition from August 22–25, 1989, when some sophisticated new technology was employed. The Remote Operated Vehicle (ROV) was a self-propelled and freely moving piece of equipment. Shipwreck expert and author Frederick Stonehouse, who witnessed the video footage as it was being recorded on this expedition, described the ROV as being "similar in concept to the CURV," but "light-years ahead in technology." It was capable of much better underwater video photography than ever before. Unlike the black-and-white images produced from the CURV's cameras, the ROV's instrumentation included 3-D color television cameras and powerful sonar scanning. Though it required great skill to operate, the ROV offered improved access to various parts as it moved around the wreck. The sonar enabled the remote operator or pilot to keep track of the ROV's position at all times. Consequently, the ROV's video footage was far superior to that obtained many years earlier from the CURV. The group effort, led by the Great Lakes Shipwreck Historical Society, included historians and researchers from the United States and Canada. National attention from the television networks was given to the venture; however, after viewing hours of videotape, a team of experts could not agree on what caused the *Fitz* to sink.

Two more underwater examinations of the *Fitzgerald* occurred in July 1994. On July 3–5, a three-person submarine called *Clelia* provided another opportunity for experts to examine the wreck site. This was only the second manned dive to examine the sunken *Fitz*. Owned by Harbor Branch Oceanographic Institution in Fort Pierce, Florida, this 22-foot, 8-ton submersible, as it is called, utilized high-technology video and still cameras to produce excellent images of the sunken vessel. Two powerful 500-watt headlamps illuminated the dark depths, creating almost daylight conditions. In addition, this amazing little submarine had the ability to hover just 18 inches above the lake's bottom, allowing for close, detailed examination. It was also equipped with an active sonar system and a versatile manipulating arm that could perform delicate tasks on the outside.

During its exploration, the *Clelia* was so dwarfed by the broken giant that at one point she unknowingly wandered into the blackness of one of the *Fitz*'s massive cargo hatches! One observer commented that seeing the wreckage buried in Superior's muddy bottom gave him an eerie, spooky feeling, like looking at a moonscape. The site was so quiet and undisturbed by currents that even the *Fitz*'s cargo of taconite pellets still lay scattered around the ship. Amazingly, after years and years under freshwater, the wreck showed little deterioration. Paint, wood, and rope were all in surprisingly good shape.

Two of the expedition's participants were Dr. Joseph MacInnis, a Canadian marine scientist who had twice investigated the famous *Titanic* shipwreck, and a maritime expert named Thomas Farnquist, considered by many to be the leading authority on the *Fitzgerald*. Farnquist, executive director of the Great Lakes Shipwreck Historical Society, had also led the 1989 ROV examination of the wreck. After the *Clelia* had completed her mission, the explorers challenged the belief that the *Fitz* broke up on the lake's surface. They saw how the bow had plowed 30 feet into the lake's bottom and concluded that, as the ship began to sink, it plunged headlong in to the depths while taking on water from massive 35-foot seas. This downward pull, combined with the momentum from the ship's powerful engines and a forward shift of the 52-million pound cargo, drove the *Fitzgerald* right into the lake's muddy bottom with tremendous force. Upon impact, the ship's center section collapsed and disintegrated, the stern violently twisted off and landed upside down, while the bow remained upright. During the three-day investigation, which included six dives, the team came across what appeared to be a sweater, coveralls, and a blanket, a touching reminder of the loss of life that will be forever linked to this tragedy.

A second expedition took place later that same month on July 26–28, and involved the *Delta*, a two-person minisubmarine owned by Delta Oceanographics in Channel Islands, California. This project was privately funded by a businessman named Fred Shannon. The *Delta*, at about 16 feet long and 4,800 pounds, was a little shorter and a lot lighter than the *Clelia*. Submersibles like the *Delta* and *Clelia* have many important uses, such as search and salvage, scientific studies, environmental studies, undersea geologic mapping, and, of course, wreck diving. The *Delta*'s photographic equipment included inside and outside video cameras (with remote control), inside and outside 35mm cameras for still photography, and strobes and lasers, as well as an array of powerful lighting intensities. Operators of the *Delta* looked out of nineteen little windows, whereas those aboard the *Clelia* viewed the wreckage through a large acrylic dome. Like the *Clelia*, the *Delta* was equipped with an arm that could be manipulated, allowing easy access for sampling and closer examination. Since submarines like these can operate at a depth of 1,000 feet, a 500-foot dive to the resting place of the *Fitz* was not unusual.

As with previous expeditions down to this wreck site, the *Delta*'s exploration attempted to unearth any clues surrounding the mysterious sinking. After three days and seven dives, the investigators reported that their videos and still photographs pointed to another theory, relating to possible earlier structural problems with the *Fitz*. According to the theory, this "structural failure" ultimately led to the *Fitz*'s breaking apart after being repeatedly battered by the rough seas.

From June 22 to July 7, 1995, at the request of the families of the lost crew, Thomas Farnquist (Great Lakes Shipwreck Historical Society), led one more expedition to plumb Superior's icy depths. A team including *National Geographic* magazine photographer Emory Kristof was organized to recover the *Fitzgerald*'s bell. The mission was the culmination of twenty years of study that revealed a changing technology. Over the course of two decades, the explorers had gone from unmanned remote vehicles to manned submersibles and finally to the bell mission's one-man NEWTSUIT.

The NEWTSUIT, invented by Canadian Phil Nuytten, is a fascinating apparatus. It is a pressurized, self-propelled, one-man diving suit with a bright yellow body and black arms and legs. Similar in appearance to an astronaut's suit, it makes the wearer look bloated and puffy. Despite its unusual and awkward appearance, however, it is a serious and sophisticated piece of diving technology. The NEWTSUIT is equipped with lighting devices on the fishbowl, bubble-faced headgear and with four propellers located about waist-high behind the diver. In addition, it has pincerlike claws for hands that the diver can manipulate. The pressurized suit allows a diver to move about freely at depths of up to 1,200 feet and offers greater mobility at a wreck site than a submersible (minisubmarine).

The plan to recover the *Fitzgerald*'s bell on July 4, 1995, included the NEWTSUIT with the assistance of two of the Canadian Navy's minisubmarines, the *SDL-1* and the *Pisces IV*. The underwater recovery was recorded from *SDL-1* using a state-of-the-art video technology called high definition video system (HDVS). HDVS produces high resolution images that are much clearer than those on an ordinary television.

The explorers knew that for the recovery mission to succeed, it would require a carefully coordinated effort between the NEWTSUIT diver and the minisubs. Attached to the ship's pilothouse at the bow (front), the bell would have to be severed from the three posts that firmly held it. More than five-hundred feet below it is very dark, so it was important to train as much light as possible on the bell. This would enable the diver to see what he was doing. The plan, therefore, involved creating a triangle that would cast three beams of light on one spot. Two points of the triangle would send out light from the *SDL-1* and *Pisces IV*. The third would come from the diver in the NEWTSUIT. All three would shine their powerful beams upon the ship's bell.

It was now time to perform the task that they had so thoughtfully planned and rehearsed. Slowly the minisubs maneuvered next to the *Fitzgerald*'s pilothouse. The brave diver in the NEWTSUIT, Bruce Fuoco, then began the dangerous task of separating the bell from the ship. Using a special torch and the clawlike manipulator "hands" at the ends of the bulging arms of the strange-looking suit, the diver was able to finally free the bell from its posts.

Family members aboard a private yacht watched with anticipation. After about three hours, the *Fitzgerald*'s 200-pound bell dramatically broke the surface, rising from Superior's treacherous depths. This must have been a bittersweet moment for the families of those who had died, for it was the first time in twenty years that anything had been recovered from the wreck site. The following day, a replica of the *Fitzgerald*'s bell, with each crew member's name engraved upon it, was placed at the underwater grave site where it serves as a memorial. The bell has since been restored to its original appearance by the Great Lakes Shipwreck Historical Society with assistance from Michigan State University.

This mission to recover the bell provided some of the best video images ever taken of the sunken ship. Although this expedition did not solve the mystery of why the *Fitz* took on so much water, vanishing without a distress signal, the explorers once again concluded that the *Fitz* sank bow first and broke apart when she hit bottom. The shoaling theory (striking bottom in shallow water near Caribou Island) assumed that damage to the hull would cause flooding that would eventually lead to sinking. However, after examining the ship's upside-down stern, the explorers found no evidence of damage from shoaling. But it is still unknown whether any such damage to the hull occurred to the disintegrated middle section or to the upright bow. Decades later, we are still left asking the same question: What caused the *Fitzgerald* to sink?

These deep-sea visitations have been heart-wrenching, painful events for all who were linked to the tragedy. Consequently, some of the family members of those who perished made a plea to the Canadian government, in whose waters the wreck resides, to officially declare this location a grave site. The family members realized that these watery depths would be the final resting place of their fathers, brothers, husbands, and sons. They would never be able to bury their loved ones on land. Some relatives, therefore, believed that the site should be off-limits to further exploration, undisturbed, just like a cemetery plot. Since graves cannot be tampered with, this marked the end of underwater investigations of the *Fitzgerald*.

On November 10, 1995, the twentieth anniversary of the tragedy, a memorial service was held at the Great Lakes

Shipwreck Museum for the families of the twenty-nine men who disappeared that stormy night. During this ceremony, the bell was rung once for each crewman. After twenty-nine haunting and lonely clangs, the bell was rung one final time to honor the memory of all sailors who have been lost on the Great Lakes. The restored ship's bell is on permanent display at the Great Lakes Shipwreck Museum at Whitefish Point, the refuge that the *Fitzgerald* had tried so desperately to reach.

• Epilogue •

Called by some the *Titanic* of the Great Lakes, the *Fitzgerald* still fascinates us. It is difficult to imagine how this mighty freighter could have vanished so dramatically from the radar screen without a call for help. For decades, the cause of the mysterious disappearance of the fallen giant has attracted much attention and debate. Although no one knows for sure what caused her to sink, books, maritime artifacts, and undersea expeditions have helped us to better understand what happened on that frightful night. Perhaps the most moving and famous tribute to the ship and her crew came in 1976, when singer/songwriter Gordon Lightfoot composed and recorded the poetic ballad, "The Wreck of the *Edmund Fitzgerald*." The song, which gained international attention, depicted the sequence of events of November 10, 1975, with remarkable accuracy.

The *Edmund Fitzgerald* has become a legend, just like the Great Lake that consumed it. Although we may never know the answers to this puzzling mystery, one thing is certain: The tragic disappearance of twenty-nine men on that terrible night will be remembered.

Explorations Down to the Wreck Site
of the *Edmund Fitzgerald*

May 20–28, 1976

U.S. Coast Guard enlisted help from U.S. Navy's Cable-controlled Underwater Recovery Vehicle (CURV III) which delivered the first pictures of the *Fitzgerald.*

September 24, 1980

Jacques Cousteau's *Calypso*, led by Jean-Michel Cousteau, sent two divers in a submarine to look at the *Fitz*'s remains in the first manned dive down to the wreck.

August 22–25, 1989

Remote Operated Vehicle (ROV) provided more video of the wreck. The expedition was led by Thomas Farnquist of the Great Lakes Shipwreck Historical Society and included members of the National Geographic Society, U.S. Fish and Wildlife Service, and Michigan Sea Grant.

July 3–5, 1994

The *Clelia*, a three-person minisubmarine owned by Harbor Branch Oceanographic Institution (Ft. Pierce, Florida), produced high-technology video and still images during a three-day expedition that involved six dives. Participants included Thomas Farnquist of the Great Lakes Shipwreck Historical Society and Dr. Joseph MacInnis, a Canadian marine scientist.

July 26–28, 1994

The *Delta*, a two-person minisubmarine owned by Delta Oceanographics (Channel Islands, CA), generated video and still images of the wreck from seven dives over a three-day period. The project was led and funded by businessman Fred Shannon.

June 22–July 7, 1995

The bell recovery mission was led by Thomas Farnquist of the Great Lakes Shipwreck Historical Society. Support for this also came from the Canadian Navy, the U.S. Coast Guard, the National Geographic Society, and the Sault Sainte Marie Tribe of Chippewa Indians. Two of the Canadian Navy's minisubmarines, the *SDL-1* and the *Pisces IV*, were used to assist Bruce Fuoco, the NEWT-SUIT diver, as he recovered the bell. The *Fitz*'s 200-pound bell was brought to the surface, and the diver placed a replica of the original bell upon the wreck as a memorial to the 29 men.

• The Crew of the Edmund Fitzgerald •

McSorley, Ernest M.	Captain	Toledo, Ohio
McCarthy, John H.	First Mate	Bay Village, Ohio
Pratt, James A.	Second Mate	Lakewood, Ohio
Armagost, Michael E.	Third Mate	Iron River, Wisc.
Holl, George J.	Chief Engineer	Cabot, Penn.
Bindon, Edward F.	First Asst. Eng.	Fairport Harbor, Ohio
Edwards, Thomas E.	Second Asst. Eng.	Oregon, Ohio
Haskell, Russell G.	Second Asst. Eng.	Millbury, Ohio
Champeau, Oliver J.	Third Asst. Eng.	Milwaukee, Wisc.
Beetcher, Frederick J.	Porter	Superior, Wisc.
Bentsen, Thomas	Oiler	St. Joseph, Mich.
Borgeson, Thomas D.	AB Maint. Man	Duluth, Minn.
Church, Nolan F.	Porter	Silver Bay, Minn.
Cundy, Ransom E.	Watchman	Superior, Wisc.
Hudson, Bruce L.	Deckhand	N. Olmsted, Ohio
Kalmon, Allen G.	Second Cook	Washburn, Wisc.
MacLellan, Gordon F.	Wiper	Clearwater, Fla.
Mazes, Joseph W.	Special Maint. Man	Ashland, Wisc.
O'Brien, Eugene W.	Wheelsman	St. Paul, Minn.
Peckol, Karl A.	Watchman	Ashtabula, Ohio
Poviach, John J.	Wheelsman	Bradenton, Fla.
Rafferty, Robert C.	Steward	Toledo, Ohio
Riipa, Paul M.	Deckhand	Ashtabula, Ohio
Simmons, John D.	Wheelsman	Ashland, Wisc.
Spengler, William J.	Watchman	Toledo, Ohio
Thomas, Mark A.	Deckhand	Richmond Hts., Ohio
Walton, Ralph G.	Oiler	Fremont, Ohio
Weiss, David E.	Cadet (Deck)	Agoura, Cal.
Wilhelm, Blaine H.	Oiler	Moquah, Wisc.

▪ Bibliography ▪

Books

Boyer, Dwight. *Ships and Men of the Great Lakes*. New York: Dodd, Mead & Co., 1977.

Hemming, Robert J. *Gales of November: The Sinking of the* Edmund Fitzgerald. Chicago: Contemporary Books, 1981.

Newcombe, Annette. *Awesome Almanac Michigan*. Fontana, Wisc.: B&B Publishing, 1993, p. 40. Created by Jean Blashfield.

Ratigan, William. *Great Lakes Shipwrecks and Survivals*. Grand Rapids, Mich.: William B. Eerdmans Publishing Co., 1977.

Stonehouse, Frederick. *Lake Superior's Shipwreck Coast*. Au Train, Mich.: Avery Color Studios, 1985.

————. *The Wreck of the* Edmund Fitzgerald. 1993. Reprint. Marquette, Mich.: Avery Color Studios, 1977.

U.S. Government Publications

U.S. Department of Transportation. *Marine Casualty Report, S.S. Edmund Fitzgerald; Sinking in Lake Superior on 10 November 1975 with Loss of Life, U.S. Coast Guard Marine Board of Investigation Report and Commandant's Action*. 26 July 1977.

Journal Articles

Askew, Timothy M. "Submersible *Clelia* Surveys Wreck of the *Edmund Fitzgerald*." *Sea Technology* 39 (December 1994): 10–13

Edwards, Jack. "The *Edmund Fitzgerald*: Playground or Sacred Ground?" *Great Lakes Cruiser*, v.2: 11, November 1995, pp.22–28.

Farnquist, Thomas. "Requiem for the *Edmund Fitzgerald*." *National Geographic* 189 (January 1996): 36–47

Stonehouse, Frederick. "The Legend Lives On." *Lake Superior Magazine* 17 (October-November 1995): 18–27

Newspaper Articles

Cleveland Plain Dealer. November 12, 15, 1975

Detroit News. July 28, 1994

Flesher, John. *"Titanic* of the Great Lakes." *Grand Rapids Press* (Michigan), July 3, 1994, pp.C1, C3

Marquette Mining Journal, (Michigan). November 11–15, 19, 21–22, December 13, 1975; November 10, December 31, 1976; September 29, November 6, 1977.

Milwaukee Journal. November 12–13, 1975

Minneapolis Star and Tribune. July 5, 1994

New York Times. November 11, 1975

Sault Evening News, (Michigan). November 11–14, 17, 18, 21, 1975; May 20–21, 1976

Brochures

Delta Oceanographics. "Delta." Brochure, n.d. Delta Oceanographics Business Office: 4500 Falkirk Bay, Oxnard, CA 93035.

Harbor Branch Oceanographic Institution. "Clelia PC 1204." Brochure, n.d. Harbor Branch Oceanographic Institution Business Office: 5600 U.S. 1 North, Fort Pierce, FL 34946.